REVELATION

REVELATION

VISIONS OF OUR ULTIMATE VICTORY IN CHRIST

PAUL YONGGI CHO

WORD PUBLISHING

Word (UK) Ltd
Milton Keynes, England

WORD AUSTRALIA
Kilsyth, Victoria, Australia

STRUIK CHRISTIAN BOOKS (PTY) LTD
Maitland, South Africa

ALBY COMMERCIAL ENTERPRISES PTE LTD
Balmoral Road, Singapore

CHRISTIAN MARKETING NEW ZEALAND LTD
Havelock North, New Zealand

JENSCO LTD
Hong Kong

SALVATION BOOK CENTRE
Malaysia

REVELATION

Copyright © 1991 by Paul Yonggi Cho.

First published in the USA by Creation House Publishers, Lake Mary, Florida.

First UK edition Word (UK) Milton Keynes, England 1992.

All rights reserved.

ISBN 0–85009–531–X (Australia ISBN 1–86258–203–3)

Scripture quotations marked NIV are from the Holy Bible, New International Version. Copyright © 1973, 1978, 1984, International Bible Society. Used by permission.

Reproduced, printed and bound in Great Britain for Word (UK) Ltd. by Cox & Wyman Ltd, Reading.

92 93 94 95 / 10 9 8 7 6 5 4 3 2 1

CONTENTS

THE REVELATION OF JESUS CHRIST

I. A GENERAL PREFACE TO THE BOOK OF REVELATION

The very first verse of the book of Revelation reveals its title. It is "the revelation of Jesus Christ." After His resurrection from the dead, when He was glorified, Jesus dictated this word of revelation to His disciple John to be given to the church He had redeemed with His precious blood.

Many people have either interpreted Revelation the wrong way or turned their faces from it. However, such an attitude is dangerous because it hinders the Word of God from growing in their lives. Since the book was recorded through the direct dictation of Jesus Christ Himself, we should receive it with godly and thankful hearts and study to understand its full meaning.

Revelation's purpose was to show God's servants that the events reserved for the last two thousand years of world history would come to pass shortly. God said He wanted this revelation taught to Christians that they might enter the eternal heaven through watchfulness and prayer. Because the book of Revelation came directly from God, we know its message is certain, for the word God speaks is always fulfilled. It's being fulfilled even now, and it will surely be fulfilled in the future. Moreover, God gave this revelation to Jesus, who in turn sent an angel to deliver it to the apostle John.

II. THE SCENE RECORDED BY
THE APOSTLE JOHN

A. The God of Trinity and the Certainty of Christ's Redemption (1:4-6)

The first things Jesus emphasized when He dictated the book of Revelation were the triune Godhead and the certainty of His redemption. "Him which is, and which was, and which is to come" mentioned by John refers to the eternal God, our Father. "The seven Spirits which are before his throne" refers to the Holy Spirit in the state of His fullness, for seven, the perfect number, was used to describe Him. In addition, John said this revelation came from Jesus Christ, "who is the faithful witness, and the first begotten of the dead, and the prince of the kings of the earth." With that, John was making it clear that this revelation came from the God of the trinity.

"[Christ] hath made us kings and priests unto God and

his Father," John wrote, and he gave glory to Christ by saying, "to him be glory and dominion for ever and ever."

After the death of the apostle Paul, many churches in gentile lands began to return to their former yoke of the law from which they had been set free. The Christian doctrine that people are saved by faith in Jesus and that salvation is purchased by His precious blood had become weakened. Many gentile converts had been persuaded to accept a legalistic faith by Jews who had come down from Judea. Those legalists taught that unless the gentile believers became circumcised and kept the days, months and holy days after the manner of Moses, they could not be saved.

Under those circumstances, John, inspired by the Holy Spirit, emphasized that people are saved not by their deeds in accordance with the law, but by the blood of Jesus, who loved them even unto death. By having John emphasize that we are made priests unto God and His kingdom, Jesus made it clear that our salvation is a divine gift of His grace.

B. The Second Coming of Jesus Christ (1:7)

The return of Jesus mentioned here is not His coming in the air but His coming to earth after the great tribulation, when those who pierced Him and everyone else will see Him. At the rapture of the church Jesus does not reveal Himself to the world but rather comes only to gather the believers as they rise to meet Him in the clouds (1 Thess. 4:17).

Jesus will come like a thief in the night and take away His chosen children, like priceless treasures, to heaven. Unsaved husbands will awake in the morning to find their wives missing, or wives will find their husbands missing. Some pilots will suddenly disappear from their aircraft. In schools, some of the teachers and pupils will be missing.

Moreover, Matthew 24:40-41 tells us, "Then shall two be in the field; the one shall be taken, and the other left. Two women shall be grinding at the mill; the one shall be taken, and the other left." Jesus' faithful believers will hear the calling of the Holy Spirit and will be taken. Though we don't know the day or the hour, it's certain our Lord Jesus' coming in the air is close at hand.

Christ's coming to earth with His saints will take place seven years after the rapture. Verse 7 says, "He [Jesus Christ] cometh with clouds." The clouds mentioned here are not ordinary clouds; these have a significant meaning. The glory of the Lord will appear like clouds, but it seems reasonable to interpret the verse as saying those clouds signify the flapping of the white robes on the saints who will return with Him.

The Bible uses the same figure of speech to describe a large number of people in Hebrews 12:1. Therefore when Jesus comes with all His saints (see 1 Thess. 3:13), with ten thousands of His saints (Jude 14), it will appear as if Jesus were coming wrapped up in the clouds.

After we've been taken up into heaven and have participated in the great wedding feast of the Lamb (see Rev. 19:6-9), we will return to earth. The site for the Lord's coming to earth the second time will be the Mount of Olives outside Jerusalem.

What does it mean that "every eye shall see him, and they also which pierced him: and all kindreds of the earth shall wail because of him"? It means the word of prophecy recorded in Zechariah 12:10 will be fulfilled: "And I will pour upon the house of David, and upon the inhabitants of Jerusalem, the spirit of grace and of supplications: and they shall look upon me whom they have pierced, and they shall mourn for him, as one mourneth for his only son, and shall be in bitterness for him, as one that is in bitterness for his firstborn."

God will give the spirit of repentance to the Jews. They
will look at the nailprints in His hands and the marks of
the spear in His side. They will recognize that this was
the Messiah whom they had reviled and crucified under
false accusations. They will weep bitterly out of contrition
and remorse. The gentiles who have lived so far according
to the lust of the flesh, the lust of the eyes and the pride
of this world (see 1 John 2:16) will likewise shed tears out
of fear of judgment and destruction.

C. The Eternity of Jesus

"The Lord" recorded in verse 8 refers to our Lord Jesus.
"Alpha and Omega" are the first and last letters of the
Greek alphabet, just as A and Z are in the English
alphabet.

Jesus is the One who was, the Creator, who existed
from the infinite past. He is not another saint who was
born two thousand years ago. Further, He is still alive,
and He is concerned for our well-being. He is constantly
interceding for us (Heb. 7:25). Out of His tender mercy
He fills all our needs. John also emphasized that He holds
the whole universe in His hands.

D. John, Who Was in the Spirit (1:9-10)

In verse 9 John identified himself. He wrote this book
of Revelation around A.D. 95. By this time the other
apostles had all been arrested, tried and martyred.

John was exiled to the Isle of Patmos. This island
swarmed with atrocious criminals who came from all
parts of the Roman empire. There was no grass or trees.
John suffered bitter insults from his fellow prisoners in
the daytime, and at night he was vexed among the felons
who quarreled with abusive words.

In the midst of such a confused and chaotic environment, however, John could still be in the Spirit through prayer. It was on one Lord's day, as he was praying, that he received Jesus' revelation.

How about you? Could you become similarly inspired? No matter how unfavorable your circumstances might be, they're probably not as bad as those of the apostle John on the Isle of Patmos. We must pray without ceasing that we may be inspired by the Holy Spirit in spite of our surroundings. Without His help, no one can understand the deep meaning of divine revelation.

First Corinthians 2:11 tells us, "For what man knoweth the things of a man, save the spirit of man which is in him? even so the things of God knoweth no man, but the Spirit of God."

Except by the Holy Spirit, no one can unveil the secrets of God. Not a word! God put John in the Spirit that He might show him His deep mysteries. Because this revelation was not written by human wisdom and experience but by the full inspiration of the Holy Spirit, it is the accurate Word of God, free from all errors as John originally penned it.

Those who recorded other books of the Bible also wrote under the inspiration of the Holy Spirit (see 2 Tim. 3:16). Therefore every verse and every word of the Scripture became the Word of God and was free from all human error.

E. The Sound of a Trumpet (1:10-16)

John wrote that when he was in the Spirit, he heard a loud voice like a trumpet. The sound meant that God was about to give him a special message.

1. The Seven Churches in Asia Minor

The great voice said, "What thou seest, write in a book, and send it unto the seven churches which are in Asia; unto Ephesus, and unto Smyrna, and unto Pergamos, and unto Thyatira, and unto Sardis, and unto Philadelphia, and unto Laodicea" (v. 11).

In those days there were more than a hundred churches in Asia Minor. Of all those churches, why did Jesus choose only seven?

First, I believe each of those many churches could identify with one of the seven, which had their own particular characteristics.

Second, through those seven types of churches, Jesus wanted to illustrate the two-thousand-year history of the church from the time of John to the present. The church age would be divided into seven periods, represented by one of the seven churches.

2. The Seven Golden Candlesticks and the Picture of Jesus

When John turned to see the voice that spoke to him, he saw seven candlesticks burning brightly. Those candlesticks were made of beaten, pure gold and signified the church, which lights up the world.

In the midst of the seven candlesticks John saw Jesus and beheld Him with a strong yearning. Previously he had thought of Jesus as being far away in a remote heaven. Now he saw the Lord right in front of him. Today Jesus is still present at our side.

Let's examine the picture of Jesus in verse 13. First, He was "like unto the Son of man," clothed with a long garment. That garment was a special article of clothing chosen by God for the high priest and the judge. Why did Jesus appear wearing such a garment? Because He is the high priest for His believers. The high priest of Israel prayed to God for the people to be blessed and forgiven for their sins. Jesus is our high priest, offering prayers that we may be forgiven of our sins and receive God's blessing.

To those who don't believe in the Lord, however, His garment becomes the special garb of a judge. Thus, our source of great blessing is a source of condemnation to unbelievers.

Second, the Scriptures tell us Jesus was "girt about the paps with a golden girdle" (v. 13). In olden times a golden girdle was worn only by the king. Thus, the girdle around Jesus' chest symbolizes His position as the King of kings.

Third, "His head and his hairs were white like wool, as white as snow" (v. 14). That means Jesus is not only pure, but also omniscient. White hair usually means one has reached the highest point of wisdom after the springs and autumns of life. However, I have observed that the younger generation today seems not to show proper respect for the aged. That is wrong. The Bible says the "hoary head is a crown of glory" (Prov. 16:31), a symbol of wisdom. Consulting with aged people, therefore, generally provides wisdom for all.

Fourth, Jesus' "eyes were as a flame of fire" (v. 14). Our hearts palpitate when a person with a pure heart, who prays a lot, looks into our eyes. Why? Because such eyes are able to penetrate the corrupt thinking we may have in our minds. How much more our hearts would palpitate if Jesus were to gaze at us with eyes like a flame of fire! His discerning eyes know and judge all hidden things.

Fifth, Jesus was standing erect, and "his feet [were] like unto fine brass, as if they burned in a furnace" (v. 15). Brass is made from copper, which throughout the Bible implies judgment. In Old Testament times the altar and fleshhooks used in sacrifices were all made from brass.

14

Our Lord says He will judge severely those who commit sin.

Sixth, the voice of our Lord is like "the sound of many waters" (v. 15). That's the voice of none other than the Creator, who speaks to us, His creation, with the same voice He used in the days of creation.

Seventh, "he had in his right hand seven stars" (v. 16). The seven stars signify the pastors of the seven churches in Asia Minor. From this verse we can understand how close pastors are to the heart of Jesus Christ. Their position is immensely honorable and high before Him. But pastors who have entered the ministry without a divine calling — perhaps through the influence of their parents, relatives or neighbors — are not the stars laid upon His palm. They're fallen stars. Those who pastor only for a profession establish numerous churches that follow a secular direction, and innumerable souls are led down a side path.

An elder of our denomination once sent me a letter in which he said he was dissatisfied with the pastor of his church and wondered what he should do. Should he drive the pastor out, or should he resist him? As far as I knew, the pastor was God's sincere servant who was carrying out a divine calling. It was true he had lots of character weaknesses, but anyone who resisted him would eventually inflict an injury upon the right hand of Jesus. As a result, that person would receive God's judgment.

In view of this, I told the elder he should choose to do one of the following: support the pastor with prayer, covering his weaknesses, or leave the church. Later I heard he had left the church. It was a wise decision.

Eighth, "out of his mouth went a sharp two-edged sword" (v. 16). The Word that proceeds out of the mouth of Jesus Christ is indeed a sword: "The word of God is quick, and powerful, and sharper than any two-edged sword, piercing even to the dividing asunder of soul and spirit, and of the joints and marrow, and is a discerner of the thoughts and intents of the heart" (Heb. 4:12). The Word is a surgical knife God uses to save our lives. When we hear and receive it, wonderful things happen to us. Our sins and wickedness will be laid bare. The devil will be cast out. Sickness and disease will be healed. Despair and heavy burdens will be removed. All these things happen because they are pierced to the dividing by the Word. Therefore it's vain to try to receive God's blessings of salvation and healing without desiring the Word or hearing it.

Ninth, Jesus' face "was as the sun shineth in his strength" (v. 16). When the cold winter passes and the warm spring comes, the sun sheds its light strongly, and everything comes to life. The full strength of sunshine means overflowing vitality. Whoever comes to Jesus will receive the shining light that radiates from His face and will be filled with the joy of the Lord to the fullest.

That same pure, kingly Jesus is here with us right now. Blessed are they who bow their knees to Him, for He will become their Shepherd and lead them down the path of abundant life.

F. Reaction of the Apostle John (1:17-18)

John was probably already past eighty years old when he saw the awesome figure of the glorified Jesus. His terror was so intense he fell at His feet as though dead.

I had a similar experience twenty years ago, when I was still a lay believer. I was fasting and praying through the night, and at about two o'clock in the morning I saw a vision. Suddenly the room filled with a bright light. Jesus was standing in front of me. When I saw that great sight, I fell down as though I were dead. I felt drained of all energy. The beating of my pulse seemed to stop. That scene remains vivid in my memory. After reading verse

17 against the backdrop of my similar experience, I can
fully understand John's reaction.

When John fell, our Lord laid His hand tenderly on him
and said, "Fear not; I am the first and the last: I am he
that liveth, and was dead; and, behold, I am alive for
evermore, amen; and have the keys of hell and of death"
(vv. 17-18).

Jesus, who died on the cross of Calvary and was resur-
rected on the third day, has the keys of death and Hades.
Therefore anyone who believes in Him does not need to
be afraid of anything, because both life and death are
under the authority of Jesus.

G. The Key to Open the
Revelation (1:19-20)

Verses 19 and 20 are keys that open John's revelation
to our understanding. When misunderstood, however,
these verses can cause one to misinterpret the whole
book. Unfortunately, that happens frequently.

> Write the things which thou hast seen, and the
> things which are, and the things which shall be
> hereafter; the mystery of the seven stars which
> thou sawest in my right hand, and the seven
> golden candlesticks. The seven stars are the
> angels of the seven churches: and the seven
> candlesticks which thou sawest are the seven
> churches (vv. 19-20).

That which the apostle John was told to record falls
into three divisions. The first is "the things which thou
hast seen." That corresponds to the first chapter of the
book of Revelation. The second is "the things which are,"
which corresponds to the period of the churches in the
second and third chapters. The third is "the things which

shall be hereafter," which corresponds to the remaining chapters (4-22). They deal with things that will unfold at the end of the church age, such as the rapture of the church to heaven, the last day of the world and the unfolding of the new heaven and the new earth.

ONE

THE CHURCH AGE

Christ's messages to the seven churches in Asia Minor were not only words of exhortation accompanied by praise and rebuke, but also words of prophecy covering the span of church history until the present time. That history falls into seven periods.

Examining the prophecy in light of what has happened, we are thrilled to find that events took place just as foretold and are still being fulfilled. Studying the second and third chapters of Revelation leads to a firm belief that this is truly the last age for the church.

Each letter to the seven churches can be divided into

six parts. First, Christ indicates the name of the recipient church. Next comes His spiritual evaluation of the church; third, His commendation; fourth, His rebuke; fifth, His exhortation; and sixth, His promise. In each letter we'll see how those things applied prophetically to the church during the past two thousand years.

I. TO THE CHURCH IN EPHESUS (2:1-7)

A. Destination

The first letter was addressed to the church at Ephesus, which was a major city in Asia Minor, a seaport and a commercial and export center. It was also the location of the great temple of Artemis (Diana). This large city was so thoroughly stirred by Paul's message that the silversmiths rioted because they believed their business of making shrines for Diana was threatened (see Acts 19:23-41). There were also many people practicing magic arts. As a result of Paul's preaching, a number of those who practiced magic arts believed in Jesus, then brought their books together and burned them (see Acts 19:13-19).

The church at Ephesus was the most privileged among all the churches because it was blessed with the best of that day's pastors. It was successively pastored by the apostle Paul, Apollos, Timothy and the apostle John. It was therefore the most trained in the Scriptures and doctrinally orthodox.

But as the church greatly expanded, thanks to its firm standing on the Word of God, it changed into an organization and became systematized. Naturally, little by little, its first love began to wane and grow cold. Prayer and praise ceased too, and the worship service leaned toward form and ritual.

B. The Description of Jesus

Many churches today have members who simply attend the services. They listen to the pastor's sermon. They're interested in things that are scientific and philosophical, and in the church ministry. But they forget the Jesus who is present. *He* is the reason for our attending and our worship. These churches typically do not lead people to feel their need to be saved, encourage them to be baptized with the Holy Spirit or pray for the sick. Therefore nobody repents. Nobody receives the Holy Spirit. And nobody is healed miraculously from disease. The works of God disappear and are replaced by human efforts. The service turns into a humanistic meeting, void of spiritual nourishment and blessing.

The church at Ephesus had become like that. At first it was a God-centered church, full of the Word and the Holy Spirit. But then the church degenerated into a humanistic body that leaned toward activity and organization. Jesus showed His insight into the church with His rebuke: "Look! I'm still walking in the midst of the seven candlesticks holding the seven stars in My right hand, but you have forgotten" (my paraphrase).

C. Commendation

The method of discipline our Lord used was always to commend first before He rebuked. Our feelings are hurt less that way, and we're more open to reprimand to correct our shortcomings. This approach is also effective in bringing up our children and in all our relationships.

Jesus commended the Ephesians because their work had been Christ-centered. They also toiled sacrificially, bearing trouble and hardships in much perseverance. He also commended their purity; they would not tolerate those who were evil. Instead, they drove the false apostles

21

out of the church.

According to Jewish tradition, the Nicolaitans referred to in verse 6 were the followers of Nicolaus, one of the first seven deacons chosen by the early church. Nicolaus, who had fallen from orthodox faith, introduced heretical Greek philosophy into the church. He held the belief that the spirit of man is good and pure, but his body is fundamentally forever evil. The spirit is by no means affected by the body's activities because the spirit is pure and holy forever. Therefore one's spirit is not affected harmfully even though one lives an unrestrained life of indulgence, drinking and eating as one wishes, living immorally. Since the spirit is purified, once a man believes in Jesus, there is no difference in his body even though it commits evil.

Many churches followed the Nicolaitans and went into corruption and licentiousness. Furthermore, the Nicolaitans systematized the church and set up a sinful hierarchy. Understandably, our Lord hated the deeds of the Nicolaitans. The church at Ephesus did too, so He commended them for that as well.

D. Rebuke

Next our Lord sharply rebuked the church by declaring, "Thou hast left thy first love" (v. 4). It was a grave problem indeed. They had learned the Word well, but while they had been busy with their many activities, including service and sacrifice and bearing hardships, they lost Jesus from their midst. What was left but form and ritual?

The situation was analogous to what can happen in a marriage relationship. When the love is lost, the husband is bound only by the duty of earning bread for his family. The wife is bound only by her duty of rearing the children and running a household. There's not a day of rest from irritation and quarrels in such a home.

The same is true in the church. Once believers' fervent relationship with Jesus has cooled off, they will just attend church on Sundays out of habit. They're going through the motions without joy or enthusiasm. How many churches today are like that? How fervent the early Christians must have been when they first believed in Jesus Christ! Doesn't the Bible say they were all filled with the Holy Spirit?

Therefore the church cannot please God unless its members maintain a constant, fervent fellowship with Christ.

E. Exhortation

Jesus exhorted the church at Ephesus to "remember...from whence thou art fallen" (v. 5). We so easily forget the blessing of the Lord. We also forget His chastisement. Jesus says "remember...from whence thou art fallen." He asks, "What happened that you now possess only a hollow faith?"

If we come to our Lord at such times, confessing what we've done and repenting, we can return once again to a fervent faith-life. Then we won't repeat the failure of the church at Ephesus.

F. Promise

Jesus promised that when the Ephesian church's first love was restored, two blessings would be given (see v. 7).

First He promised paradise. This paradise is far better than the one where Adam and Eve lived. The new paradise will be in heaven. Christ will transform our bodies from their former state of dishonor to a glorious new state; from weakness to power; from the natural to the spiritual so that these mortal bodies will put on immortality, and we will live forever with Him.

Second, He promised He would give the fruit of the tree of life. That fruit isn't given just for the pleasure of seeing, but also for nourishment.

G. Interpretation of the Prophecy (A.D. 33-100)

The letter to the Ephesian church represents the apostolic church in the period from A.D. 33 to 100. The name *Ephesus* means "to relax or let go." Hence, the name implied that love had departed, and only form and rituals were left.

The church of Christ, which had been red-hot with the fire of the Holy Spirit in its initial stages following His ascension, slowly lost its first love. By the year 100 it had turned into a church with nothing more than forms, like the Ephesian church.

What will happen to a church that has lost its first love if it doesn't repent and return to the Lord? God will visit it with chastisement, as we'll see in the next letter.

II. TO THE CHURCH IN SMYRNA (2:8-11)

A. Destination

Jesus' second letter was addressed to the church in Smyrna, a seaport forty miles north of Ephesus. This flourishing city was situated on the trade route linking Rome to India through Persia, so commerce developed rapidly. Smyrna was founded by Alexander the Great and had temples erected to the sun god, Zeus. It was also the center of emperor worship and had temples honoring Roman rule.

B. The Description of Jesus

Jesus appeared to the church at Smyrna as the One who was the first and the last; who had been dead and was now alive. He said (paraphrase), "You shall also suffer death and affliction." But He added, "I am the first and the last, so leave everything to Me. As I was dead and am now alive, so you shall be alive even though you die, if you believe in Me." Through this saying Jesus was foretelling the severe persecution that would come to the church at Smyrna.

C. Commendation

Our Lord always commends the church under persecution. His saying can be paraphrased thus: "Though outwardly you look very poor because you're under persecution, actually you are not so. The truth is that you're rich." Tribulation and affliction always purify our faith.

Corrie ten Boom, the famous Dutch revivalist, was delivered from the point of death in one of the Nazi concentration camps of World War II. Following is one of her testimonies.

In the U.S.S.R., Christianity was under such severe persecution that believers worshipped in secret places like warehouses or underground rooms. One day while the Christians were holding a secret service in a warehouse, several soldiers of the Russian Army, armed with submachine guns, kicked the door open and raided the place in the middle of a service. All the Christians held up their hands at gunpoint. In the Soviet Union, those who were discovered holding worship services were sent to Siberia, a place of endless suffering and agony.

Then the soldiers said, "You shall be tried summarily at an appointed place. If any of you want to disown Jesus

Christ, step forward. Now is your chance to avoid persecution."

Some people stood up and went out. Most of the people, however, turned pale but stood still. They had to decide whether to die for Jesus' sake or to flee like the others. The silence was deadening as the soldiers waited.

Once more the soldiers shouted, "We will give you one more chance. If any of you want to live, come out quickly. Those of you who still 'stick to Jesus,' prepare yourself now for death!"

Nobody moved a muscle. Then the believers all lowered their hands and began to pray, readying themselves to die.

At that point, the soldiers bolted the doors of the warehouse and turned around. Throwing their rifles to the floor, they said, "Brothers, we are Christians, too! We have come here to attend the worship service. We had to behave like that because we were afraid there might be some false Christians among you. Since the false believers have all fled, we do not need to worry about detection. Now let's continue the service!"

Hallelujah! As you can see from that true story, you can always distinguish sham from the genuine. And when Christ said to the church at Smyrna, which was under persecution, "Thou art rich," He meant spiritual richness.

The Lord also commended the Christians at Smyrna for overcoming the blasphemy they received from the Jews. Since Smyrna was a center of emperor worship, anybody who would not bow down and worship the emperor was in danger of death. Many Jews were executed for their monotheistic faith, and while being pulled to death they dragged the Christians to the same death out of hatred. Thus were many Christians at Smyrna executed. Jesus said it wasn't the Jews but Satan who worked behind them.

26

D. Rebuke

Like the church at Philadelphia, the church at Smyrna received no rebuke, as Smyrna's sufferings had helped to keep the believers pure in faith and life.

E. Exhortation

The Lord exhorted the church at Smyrna to be faithful unto death. Jesus said He would be their guarantor and give them a crown of life. Since we're also guaranteed by the Lord Jesus Christ, we shall also be taken care of if we have been faithful to the Lord, whether we live or die.

F. Promise

The Lord promised the church at Smyrna it would not be hurt at the second death. The first death is the death of the body, and the second is the death of the soul. The first death comes to every being on this earth, but the second death, signifying the death of the wicked in the next world, is identified as everlasting torment of the soul in the lake of fire burning with brimstone. That has no power over the faithful. This promise means that even though the church at Smyrna was being put to death by the Roman persecutors, the Lord guaranteed it would avoid the second death and be translated to heaven.

G. Interpretation of the Prophecy (A.D. 100-312)

The church at Smyrna characterizes the church from A.D. 100 to 312, when Christianity was officially recognized by Constantine the Great. The church of this period was under severe persecution.

The name *Smyrna* means "crushed myrrh." Imagine!

Myrrh is a bitter-tasting preservative, so wouldn't crushed myrrh taste even more bitter? It was a prophetic name that foretold how terrible the persecution would be for the church there.

The church at Smyrna follows the church at Ephesus. Don't forget that when love waned at the Ephesian church, the judgment of God followed. Through persecution and tribulation God restores the pure first love to the church.

The Bible says the church at Smyrna would have tribulation for ten days (see v. 10). This signified that ten Roman emperors would persecute the church.

The first was the notorious Nero, who reigned in Rome from A.D. 37 to 68. He was sixteen years old when he ascended the throne, and he killed his wife, Octavia, and his mother and put all his brothers to death. Tradition says that after he committed those horrible crimes, he wanted to write a poem. However, when no poetic inspiration came into his mind, he was suddenly possessed with a wild desire to see the city of Rome aflame, and he ordered it set on fire.

The entire city was engulfed in flames, and the citizens were dying with agonizing cries. Nevertheless, in the midst of this hellish conflagration Nero was enjoying himself by writing a poem. The truth began to circulate that the fire had been started by the emperor, so he concocted a false rumor that the Christians were responsible and ordered their arrest.

Many Christians were imprisoned and executed because of this. In A.D. 67 Peter, the chief of the disciples and a pillar of the early church, was arrested and died a martyr's death. It is said he was crucified upside down at his own request because he felt himself unworthy to be put to death in the same manner as his Master.

In A.D. 68, the year following Peter's martyrdom, Paul also became a martyr. According to tradition, Paul was beheaded.

Thus, during the persecution of Nero, the two most prominent figures of the early church died.

The second persecution occurred from A.D. 81 to 96 during the reign of Domitian. He ordered the people to worship him as the god Jupiter. Under his persecution the apostle John was exiled to the Isle of Patmos, where he wrote the book of Revelation.

The third persecution arose during the reign of Trajan. He outlawed the Christian faith and persecuted the church from A.D. 98 to 117. During this period, tradition says that Ignatius, the chief disciple of Peter, was thrown into a den of lions, where he was torn into pieces.

The story goes that a judge urged Ignatius to betray Jesus, but the disciple, who was more than eighty years old, refused.

He answered, "I have believed in Jesus from my youth until today. He has never betrayed me even once. How can I betray Him now?"

When such heroic martyrdom occurred in the amphitheater, the grace of Jesus Christ touched the hearts of the onlookers. They were so greatly moved that they were converted. Christianity is like a burning bonfire. The more you strike it with a stick, the more sparks will fly in all directions, starting thousands of new fires.

The fourth persecution occurred during the reign of Marcus Aurelius, who was on the throne from A.D. 161 to 180. He was a philosopher who tried to restore the Roman ideal of self-reliant, stoic virtue and the old state religion. The emperor martyred (among many others) Polycarp and Justin.

The fifth persecutor was Septimus Severus, who reigned from A.D. 202 to 211. He enacted a rigid law against the spread of Christianity. As a result, the father of Origen, North Africa's renowned theologian, was beheaded.

The sixth persecutor was Maximum, who reigned from A.D. 235 to 237. He was a rude barbarian who massacred the Christians and had their bodies buried together in lots of fifty and sixty.

Emperor Decius reigned from A.D. 249 to 253 and persecuted the church fiercely, intending to destroy it. Fortunately, God caused him to die at an early age.

The next ruler to persecute the church was Valerian, who reigned from A.D. 257 to 260. During his persecution Cyprian, the bishop of Carthage and a renowned Christian author, died a martyr's death.

The ninth persecutor was Aurelian, who reigned from A.D. 270 to 275.

The last persecutor was Diocletian, who ruled from A.D. 303 to 312. He issued edicts causing the Christian churches to be destroyed and all copies of the Bible to be burned. His persecution was so extensive and violent throughout the entire Roman Empire that Diocletian erected a monument commemorating the termination of Christianity. Twenty-five years after his death, however, Christianity became the state religion of Rome.

Thus, ten persecutors tried in vain to destroy Christianity throughout the years from 100 to 312. Christianity never did die completely, and the prophecy "ye shall have tribulation ten days" was fulfilled.

During that period the church went underground to avoid capture. The underground galleries called catacombs still remain in Rome. I once entered a catacomb, following a guide. It seemed like a labyrinth with long, winding tunnels. It seemed to me that there would be no possible way out.

The catacombs had enough space for places of worship. Additionally, their perpendicular walls contained small compartments that had been cut out to bury the dead. On the walls of these tombs, pictures were drawn of a bird and the face of Jesus with the following inscription: "Our beloved resurrects and goes to the presence of the Lord. Wait for the coming of the Lord." The symbolism meant that the soul flies away like a bird and goes to the throne of Jesus Christ.

I was greatly moved to see joy and hope in the epitaphs and pictures the Christians had left behind rather than the shadow of sorrow. For more than two centuries numerous Christians were born in those dark catacombs. But they never gave up the staunch hope they cherished in their hearts for a bright tomorrow.

To those spiritual warriors who kept their faith under persecution and handed it down to us, we owe our freedom to hear and read and preach the gospel.

Sometimes we're frustrated and prone to complain at small hardships and afflictions. I pray in the name of the Lord Jesus, however, that you and I will look at those heroes of the faith and become victorious warriors ourselves by overcoming tribulation and persecution with boldness.

III. TO THE CHURCH IN PERGAMOS (2:12-17)

A. Destination

Jesus' third letter was addressed to the church in Pergamos. In those days Pergamos was the capital of Asia Minor and a flourishing center of politics, power, heathen worship and learning. It had temples to Zeus and altars offered to Aesculapius, its tutelary god. The people put serpents on their altars and worshipped them. Moreover, the cult of emperor worship flourished here too. It was the duty of every citizen to burn incense once a year to his deified image.

B. The Description of Jesus

The Lord appeared to the church in Pergamos as "he which hath the sharp sword with two edges" (v. 12). Because this church "hast there them that hold the doctrine of Balaam...to eat things sacrificed unto idols, and to commit fornication" (v. 14), it needed to repent, or He would come in judgment. With the sword of the Word (v. 12; see Heb. 4:12), the Lord will reveal and sever false doctrine.

C. Commendation

Jesus commended the church in Pergamos for keeping its pure faith and not compromising with heresies. He especially pointed out a man named Antipas. Tradition relates this concerning the martyrdom of Antipas:

At that time emperor worship was in full force. One day a Roman official took Antipas before the image of the emperor and said, "Antipas, worship the image."

Antipas answered, "The King of kings and the Lord of lords is Jesus Christ only, so I will not worship any other god. Only Jesus."

The Roman official was infuriated and shouted, "Antipas, don't you know that all the world is against you?"

Antipas responded, "Then I, Antipas, acknowledge Jesus as the Lord of lords against all in the world."

Enraged at this answer, the official ordered some men to heat up a brazen bull, and Antipas was put into it. There he was slowly roasted to death. Yet he never denied Jesus.

D. Rebuke

Jesus also rebuked the church in Pergamos, saying, "Thou hast there them that hold the doctrine of Balaam"

(v. 14). When the children of Israel came out of Egypt and entered the land of Canaan, Balak, king of Moab, called Balaam, the prophet, and asked him to curse Israel. Balaam, whose eyes were darkened by power and money, advised Balak that if the Moabites tempted the Israelites with fornication, God would destroy them (see Num. 25:1-9; 31:16). So Balak had beautiful Moabite women dance lewdly on the altars of the idol, and the men of Israel committed fornication with the women of Moab and worshipped the idol. As a result, God's judgment came upon them, and thousands of people died in a single day.

The church in Pergamos harbored fornicators, and the Christian church of that day committed spiritual fornication by joining itself with the Babylonian religion.

The Lord also rebuked the church in Pergamos for including some who held the doctrine of the Nicolaitans. As previously explained, the Nicolaitans were the followers of Satan. They introduced Greek philosophy into the church and also caused it to commit fornication and adultery.

E. Exhortation

Jesus exhorted the church, "Repent; or else I will come unto thee quickly, and will fight against them with the sword of my mouth" (v. 16). From this we know how indignant He was. The church He bought with His own blood was tainted with heresy and immorality.

F. Promise

He promised, however, that He would give the hidden manna to the person who repented and overcame temptation. This hidden manna is heavenly, spiritual food — Jesus Himself.

He also promised He would give a white stone to those who overcame. This refers to the stone the court of that day gave as a token to accused criminals when they were found not guilty. (If they were found guilty, they were given a black stone.) Therefore Jesus was promising that when people repented, He would forgive their sins and make them righteous. The promise extends to us as well. Hallelujah!

G. Interpretation of the Prophecy (A.D. 312-590)

Prophetically, the church in Pergamos refers to the church period from A.D. 312, when Constantine the Great proclaimed Christianity as Rome's state religion, until the year 590.

Pergamos means "marriage." While Constantine made Christianity the state religion, he also took advantage of it politically. He used the marriage of state and church (including the incorporation of the Babylonian religion's heresy) to consolidate the empire's unity.

Accordingly, in the annals of church history the church in Pergamos represents the adulterous church that compromises with the world. When suffering persecution, they become pure. But when they receive blessings again, they compromise with the world, turning into Pergamos and falling to depravity in pursuit of worldly pleasure.

IV. TO THE CHURCH IN THYATIRA (2:18-29)

A. Destination

The fourth letter is addressed to the church in Thyatira, a little city in Asia Minor. The chief industry of this city was fabric dyeing. Fortune-telling was also prevalent, and numerous people would gather for this purpose in a large temple.

B. The Description of Jesus

Jesus was described to the church in Thyatira as having "eyes like unto a flame of fire, and his feet are like fine brass" (v. 18). He penetrates reality with those eyes and judges the church with those feet.

C. Commendation

The Lord commended the works, love, service, faith and patient endurance of the church in Thyatira (see v. 19).

D. Rebuke

In verse 20, however, the Lord also issued a severe rebuke citing the church's tolerance of Jezebel, the false prophetess. Jesus was referring to a woman fortune-teller in Thyatira, who even went into the church to practice her evil, but symbolically He was referring to the Jezebel of the Old Testament. She was the daughter of Ethbaal, king of the Zidonians, and Ahab, king of Israel, took her to be his wife (see 1 Kin. 16:29-33). She brought the worship of Baal into Israel and had the altars of the Lord God demolished.

In Seoul, Korea, alone, more than six hundred pseudo-churches practice fortune-telling. What they have received is not the Holy Spirit but the spirit of a mountain god, a demon.

Jesus rebuked the spiritual adultery of this church that followed Jezebel, mixing faith and divination.

E. Exhortation

The Lord gave the church in Thyatira the exhortation that it should not compromise with the shamanistic faith but stand firm on the Word (see vv. 24-25). Our faith also should be based firmly on the Word. Extravagant fondness for prophecy — an obsession with details not revealed in the Bible — might lead your faith astray just as in the case of the church in Thyatira.

F. Promise

Jesus promised He would give power over the nations and the morning star to him who overcomes temptation (see vv. 26-28). The morning star signifies the second coming of Jesus Christ. If we stand firm on the Word with pure faith, we will have the privilege of taking part in the second coming of Christ.

G. Interpretation of the Prophecy (A.D. 590-1517)

Thyatira means "continued sacrifice," which the Catholic mass is all about. In terms of church history, Thyatira signified the Dark Ages of the church from 590 to 1517, when Martin Luther began the Reformation. After Christianity became the state religion of the Roman empire, the church grew steadily more worldly. It left the true nature of the faith — the religion of the Word, praise and prayer. Lay people attending services only watched what was going on, the priests offering sacrifices. Consequently, the faith of the laity atrophied into little more than spectating at rituals.

One of the abominable practices adopted by the church was the selling of indulgences to collect contributions from the believers. It was a last unbiblical resort to